EMBROIDERY
from sketch to stitch

EMBROIDERY
from sketch to stitch

Pat Langford

Kangaroo Press

Acknowledgments

Thanks to:
• My family, who are always there for me—Martin, Cheryllee, Tim and Emma.
• Fred and Elinor Wrobel, who encouraged me to exhibit.
• Toni Valentine, for taking so many photographs for me.
• Jackie Macdonald, who kindly did the typing for me.
• Heather Joynes, who encouraged me to submit this book.
• And a big thank-you to all the friends who have allowed me to draw in so many different situations.

EMBROIDERY FROM SKETCH TO STITCH

First published in Australia in 1996 by Kangaroo Press
An imprint of Simon & Schuster (Aust.) Pty Ltd
20 Barcoo Street, East Roseville NSW 2069

Paperback edition printed 2000

A Viacom Company
Sydney New York London Toronto Tokyo Singapore

© Patricia Langford 1996

National Library of Australia
Cataloguing-in-Publication data
A CIP catalogue record for this book is
available from the National Library of Australia

ISBN 0 7318 1008 2

Set in Sabon 11.5/15 pt.
Printed in Hong Kong through Colorcraft Ltd

10 9 8 7 6 5 4 3 2 1

Contents

£1

Introduction

Embroidery is my passion; no other artistic medium gives me the same satisfaction, the tactile and visual pleasure. Even though I am happy working in other media, nothing else has embroidery's wonderful variety of texture, the feel of the threads and fabric, the richness of surface and intensity of colour, the lateral spread into related techniques.

Everything around me speaks to me in shapes and colours. No matter where I am, I am never without sketchbook and pens, I can never stop myself from doing one more drawing. I have been very fortunate to have done a lot of travelling, sometimes on holiday, sometimes through my teaching. It has become accepted by my hosts that I will always have a sketchbook in my hand—in the kitchen, in the garden, in the car, anywhere. I use Pentel pens and Texta colours most of the time. (It's not a good idea to use paint in someone else's car or house!) If I am on a special painting trip, however, I like to work large, with crayons and inks, and tubes of paint.

My sketchbooks have been the source of my embroidery for quite some time. A camping trip to the Flinders Ranges, organised by a group of friends also interested in painting and photography, led to the first body of work in this book, from the exhibition 'The Flinders—Works on Fabric' at Woolloomooloo Gallery in 1990. A print-making friend and I shared the excitement of sketching from the moment we stepped on the bus. We never put our pens down while there was light to see by. The joy of sitting and painting for a whole day in that wonderful landscape was immense; the contrasts of colour, the changing landscape, the formation of the rocks, the unbelievable richness everywhere I looked, completely bowled me over. Six thousand kilometres of road with such a quantity of material to record was almost too much to take in.

At that time I was exploring the possibilities in the combination of silk painting with embroidery. This turned out to be the perfect way of translating the Flinders into fabric and thread, although I did have to work my way through several processes to realise the best method of working. During this period I kept very closely to the drawings and paintings in my sketchbook.

The second exhibition, 'Journeys', at the Woolloomooloo Gallery in 1992, came together after a year of contrasts, seeing many different places and meeting many different people—including the Olgas, Kakadu and the Centre itself. Here the colours exploded in my head. I had to find a new collection of fabrics and threads to reveal the character of the Olgas—reds, oranges and more reds.

The year began with a trip to another favourite place — across the Tasman, driving and drawing among the wonderful mountains and lakes of New Zealand. Here there was a completely different set of forms and colours to register.

As I travel I come to the safe havens of the houses where my friends have created their own space and comforts. Each house asks for a different technique to say something about its particular qualities. A friend in Sydney bought an older style house with deep-set windows and leadlights giving a new quality to the light. An intimate approach was needed here, in the series *Yolande's Windows*, with gold kid creating a very different scale.

It seems to me that embroiderers are almost always gardeners as well as stitchers. New Zealanders are no exception with their walled gardens, masses of pot plants, bushes and banks of flowers, often seen through the most interesting windows. The gardens and interiors needed something new. Of all things, the blanket that had been sitting in the studio managed to come together one day with a group of glittery fabrics and puff paints.

In the U.K. I was mesmerised by the endlessly changing landscape of my own West Country, with its patterned fields and hedgerows, the narrow roads with plant-covered walls, and trees making green tunnels to travel through. Each county has its own colours, of stone and earth and buildings, right up to the Hebrides, almost another world with that thin layer of earth just resting on top of the rock.

Roses in full bloom dominated the scene in the small gardens and the public gardens of Britain, especially the climbing roses that go as high as a house.

The last group of work comes from the exhibition 'Celebration' at Woolloomooloo Gallery in 1994, based on two trips to the United Kingdom and more travels around Australia. Back in the U. K. once again I was taken by the delight of standing in the National Gallery amongst old friends like Giotto, Piero della Francesca, Seurat, Picasso. I was overwhelmed by all the gold surface in early works, by the wealth of decoration in the Victoria and Albert and the British Museum. Gold, the symbolic colour of ornament, became the starting point for this last group.

Sitting and talking in a friend's house one day (perhaps

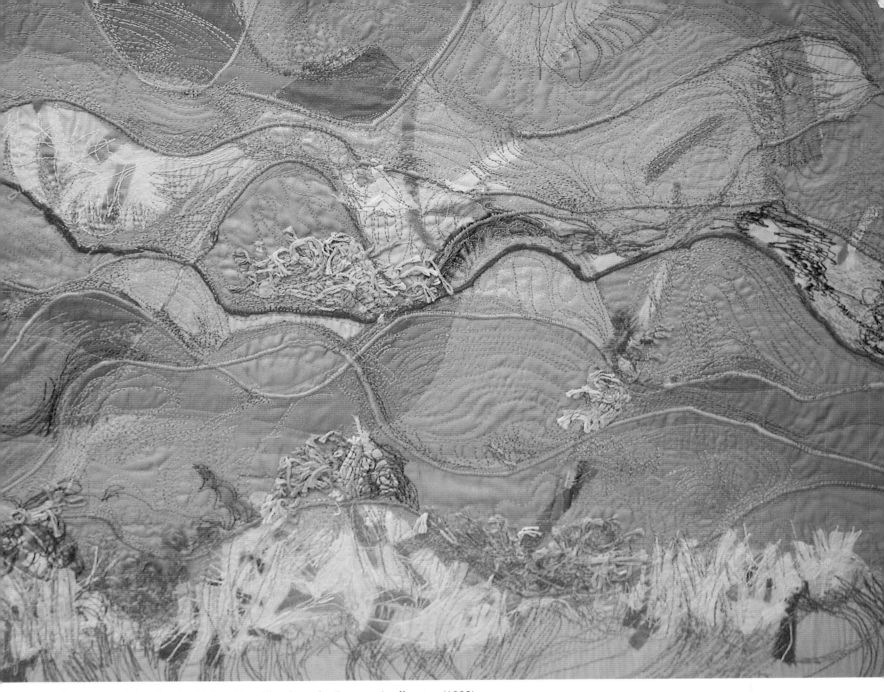

Detail from *That Special Light of the Olgas* from the 'Journeys' collection (1992)

not really listening) my mind was drifting over new shapes to frame this group of works when my eyes lit on a row of plates hanging on the wall in the next room . . . perfect shapes, complete, with no need for framing. I realised how many drawings in the sketchbooks would fit this format.

Although I drew the new designs in great detail before I started embroidering, this collection snowballed into many new directions as it went along. Groups in restaurants, scenes at the theatre and the opera, on the pier at Eastbourne, the Arts Centre restaurant in Perth in Western Australia, barges at Stratford, fruit on a platter . . .

Everything around us can be the start of a new piece of work. In this book I wish to share with you the constant enjoyment I find in looking at the world around me and the pleasure I have in translating it into fabric and thread.

Pat Langford
1996

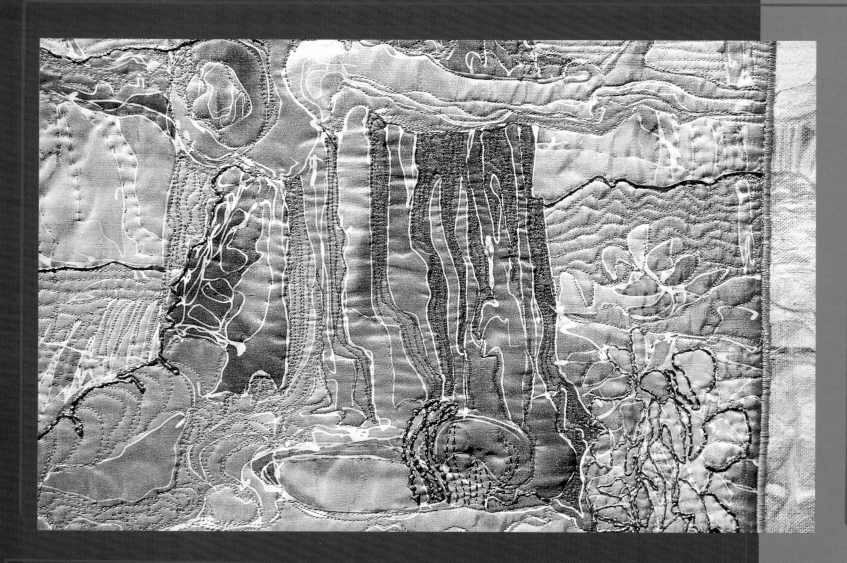

The Magic Tree

The Magic Tree was a key work of the exhibition based on my trip to the Flinders. In this work I explored feelings and impressions I had after walking and drawing in the grandeur of the landscape. The internal walls seemed constantly to be making new images with changing shapes and colours. At this time I was very involved with silk painting as such a drawing technique, which helped me to create the detail of the bark with the richness of the colours of the gees till saving through this series of works I found myself making very close reference to the original drawings this piece set the style for the work in the exhibition.

This piece sh...
one more ste...
collection of...
quilted in...
pieces which...
added to th...
of silk which...
to the final...
we set up ca...
in the Flinde...
the sun was...
quickly put...
down on pa...
constantly...
colour addin...
variables to th...
patterns of th...
tonal quac...
changed a...
clouds in fron...
sunset cast...
across the l...

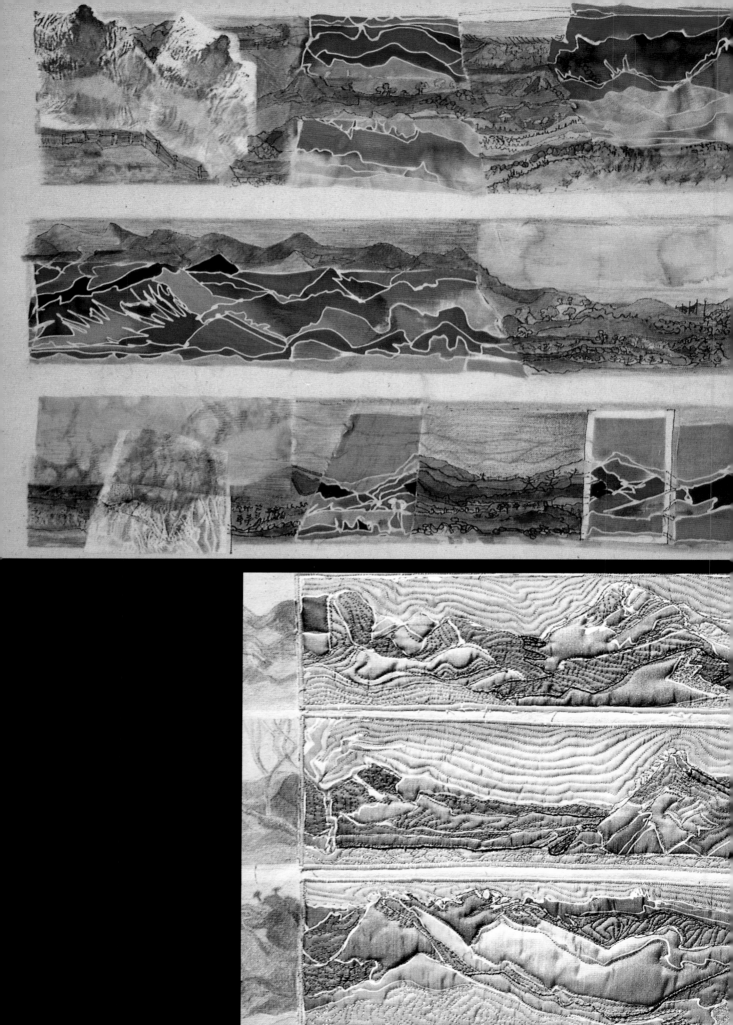

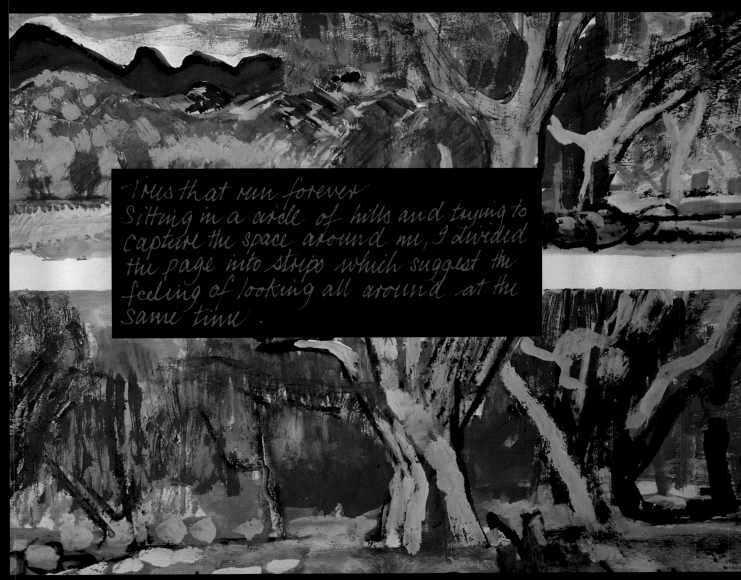

Trees that run forever
Sitting in a circle of hills and trying to
capture the space around me, I divided
the page into strips which suggest the
feeling of looking all around at the
same time.

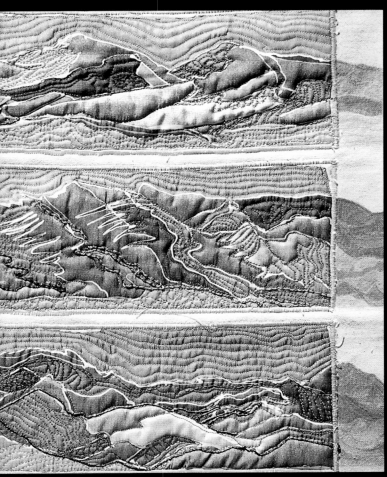

How can I take in so Much?
This much larger work evolved from
a day spent at the bush camp at Dingley
Dell, where we enjoyed the luxury of a
whole day's painting at one spot. Canopied
by the river I had the joy of being able
to sketch many parts of it. The river
wound in amongst many islands
of fascinating rocks. There were
stepping stones to cross the river and
luxuriant growth underneath
the trees.

Suggestions of Light.
Many works were on
paper. I attempted to
treat the combination
of paper and fabric in
this picture in a variety
of ways. This piece
has used torn and
rolled etching paper,
curling the edges as
a reminder of the
dark stripping from
the tree. I wanted to
emphasize the light
of the early morning.

Suggestion of Light

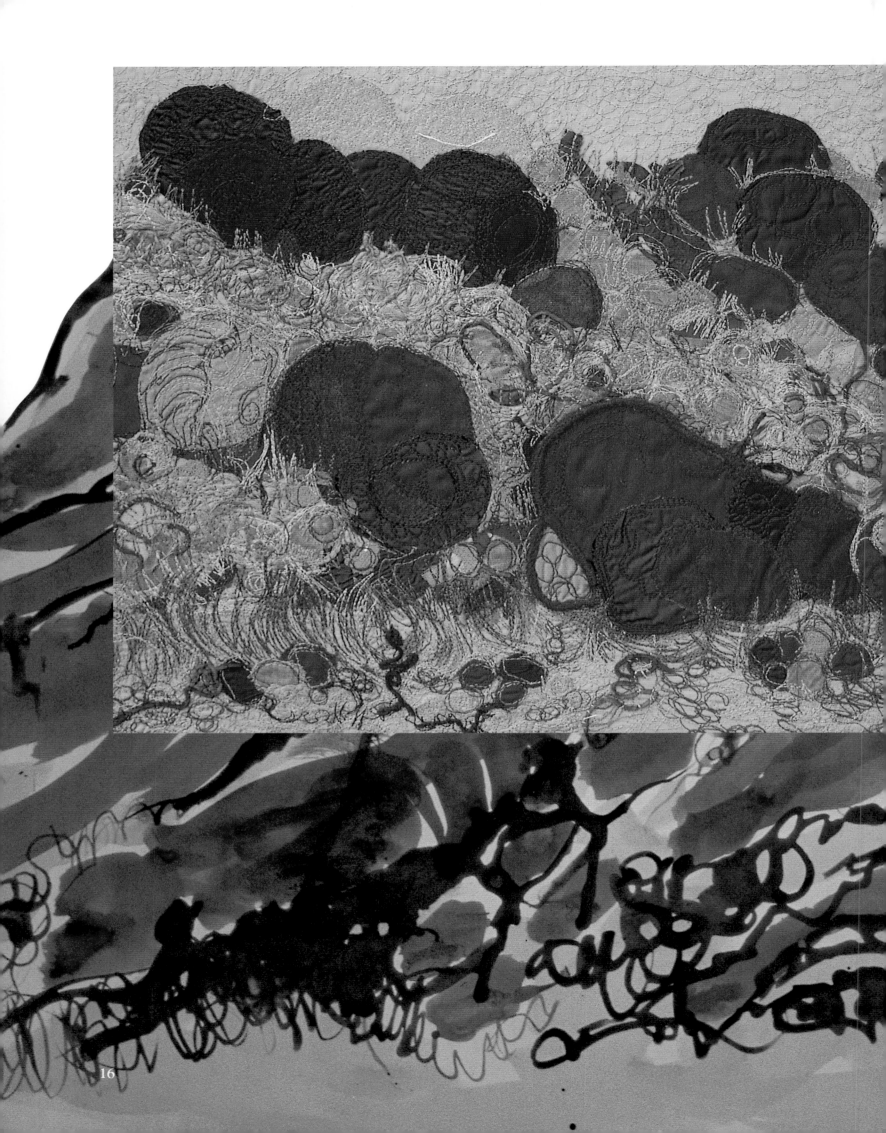

Reds of the Olgas

These are some of the works from the second exhibition, which were based around a trip to the Centre and to Kakadu — an absolutely breathtaking experience, with so much colour.

The many reds of the Olgas are just overwhelming. Being formed of conglomerate the same oval shapes are found everywhere: even the mountains are like large pebbles. I was very conscious of smaller rocks looking as though they had just fallen away from the larger rocks or broken from the hills themselves. All the drawings had to be in colour, using a variety of techniques such as coloured inks, poster colours and acrylics. Many were drawn directly with the tube of paint.

Finding a way to interpret all this meant searching for a completely new collection of fabrics. I used a very quiet green as background, and added rich reds, oranges and pinks in many different textures.

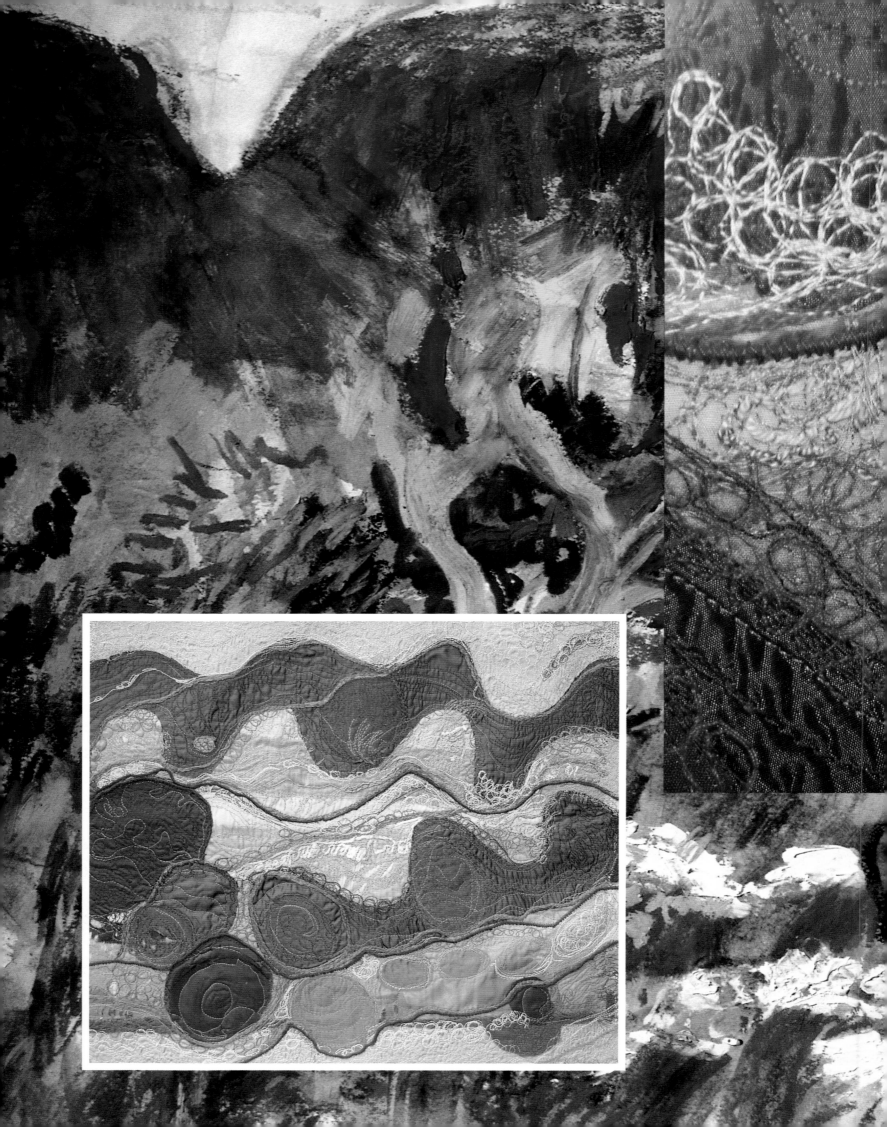

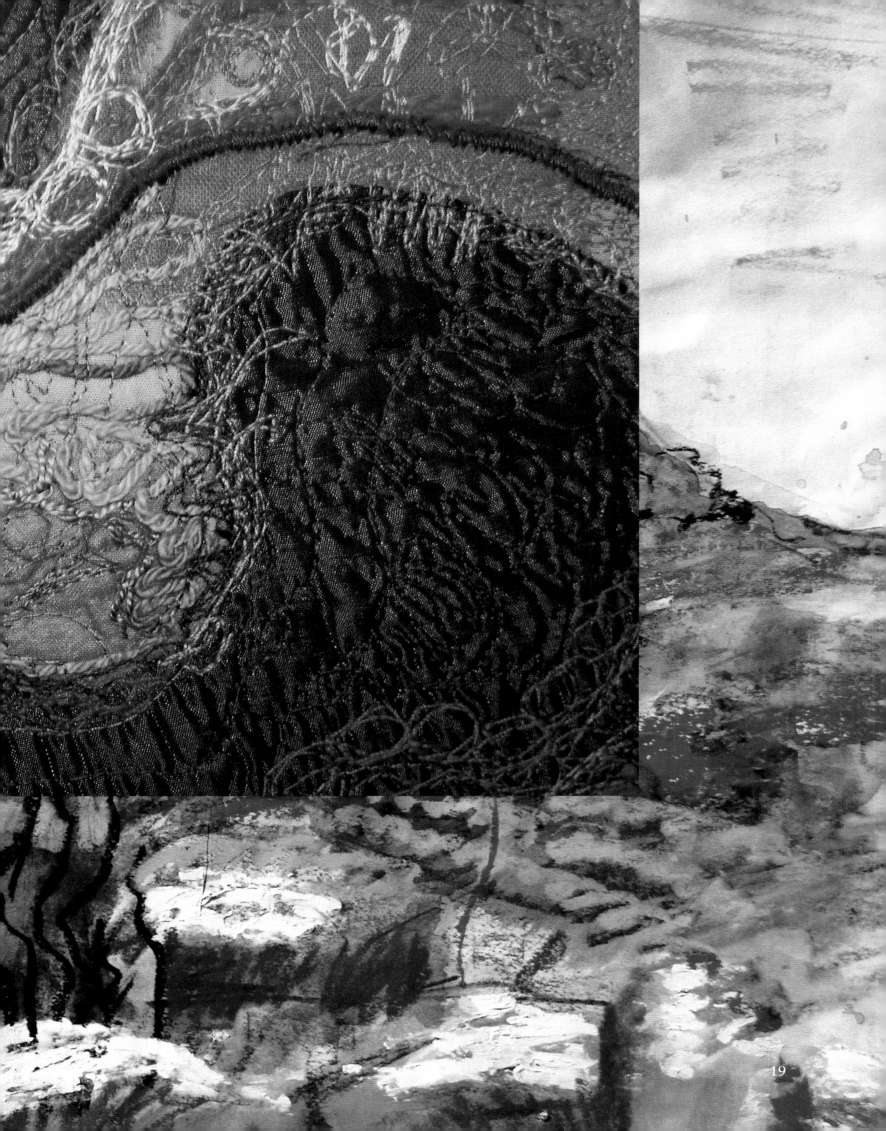

Timber creek
Moving on to Timber creek, a wonderful spot
with a campsite just beside the river where the
guide insisted there was a crocodile just
here in the water. Recording the trees and river
from every angle called for a technique which
conveyed the depths of the tree layers. Here
I used reverse appliqué

Three Drawings

Each set
to lean th

ter-Fall Creek, a series of rock pools.

this is an exploss

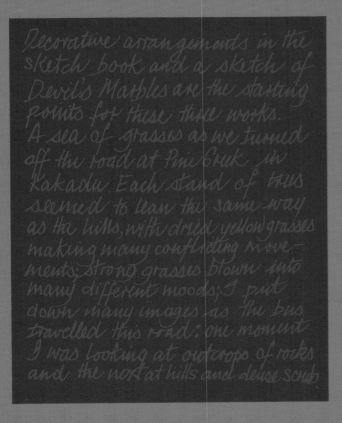

Decorative arrangements in the
sketch book and a sketch of
Devil's Marbles are the starting
points for these three works.
A sea of grasses as we turned
off the road at Pine Creek in
Kakadu. Each stand of trees
seemed to lean the same way
as the hills, with dried yellow grasses
making many conflicting move-
ments; strong grasses blown into
many different moods; I put
down many images as the bus
travelled this road: one moment
I was looking at outcrops of rocks
and the next at hills and dense scrub

...... gold

...... the aborigine didn't burn off until near the wet season to kill
...... is third largest populated area in N.T.   ground quickly
...... are such an obvious form of transport, mostly 2 trailers
...... limestone as we leave Katherine.   the bark.
...... are grass, ant hills and dry red soil, still.
.... into the towns. We seem to see them everywhere

Pink Light at Waterfall

This work developed from photographs as well as the usual drawings. We had set up camp and painted around the waterfall all day. There was a large pool at the foot of a set of cascades. If you climbed the hill there were more waterfalls and a river that seemed to go nowhere. Every thing was covered in red dust from bushfires in the park.

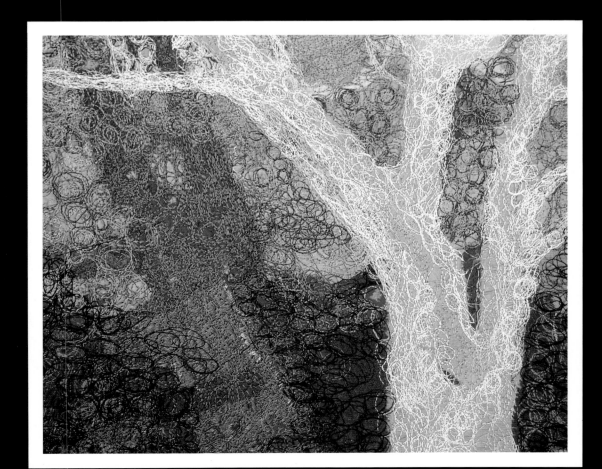

Spinifex Circle

The spinifex grass grows in wonderful roundish shapes, enlarging year by year as the centre dies out. The formations can vary greatly, some growing as rings and some as domes. It is very easy to see why marsupial mice favour spinifex for their homes. The mystery of the contained spaces of the spinifex circle seemed to be suggested by small contained works.

Yolande's Windows

A dear friend moved into a wonderful old house
with deep set windows that made me feel I
could just curl up in them. There were beautiful
stained glass windows and decorated ceilings.
The Kitchen window with the stained glass
started a whole new series I tried to capture the
intimate quality of the space by creating small
rich works with a combination of gold kid,
metal threads, paper and paint.

Kitchen Window

The shiny surfaces of paintwork, pots
and glasses are illustrated in this
piece using the simple richness of
gold kid as a foil to the mass of
detail

Glitter
Also
precious
kid as
to offset
stitchery

in the window
exploits the
quality of gold
a background
the mass of

After the Party
Suggests the emptiness of the
house when everyone has left

31

Double Image
I mounted two windows
side by side to make
this special image. The
gold machine stitching
and the final overlay
of gold leaf link the
works together, the two
images revealing two
moods at the same
time.

Deep Window

The dark blue paper emp
the depth of the window

Through the Hatch

Interiors and windows are always fascinating in
their revelations of the human touch and influence
on the environment. The sketches for these panels
suggested a new direction which materialized
through an unusual combination of materials.
Blanket, puff paint and organza came together
in a soft layered technique with many subtle
colour changes.

34

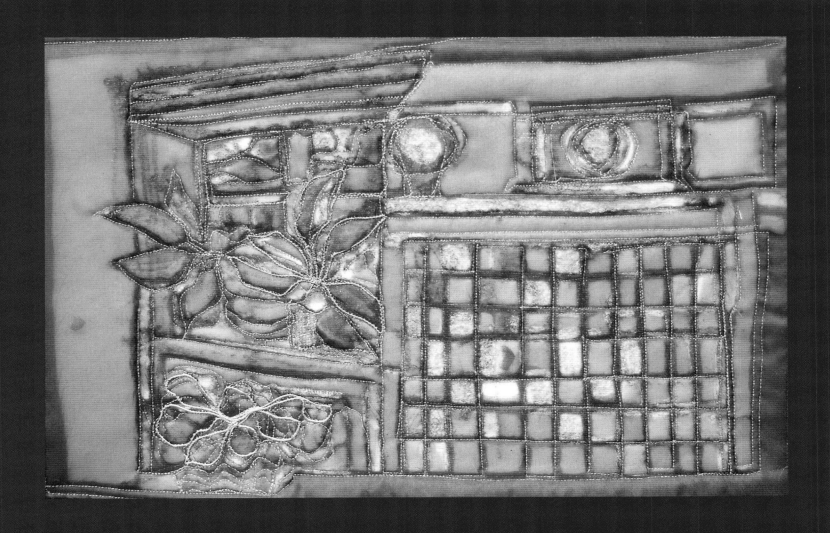

Corner of the Lounge Room
used the same technique
but reversed the colour
arrangement.

35

New Zealand's Gardens
Embroiderers are all good
gardeners, resulting in New
Zealand's being some of the
finest. I have been fortunate
enough to stay with some of
these embroiderer-gardeners'
and had the twin pleasures
of enjoying their gardens and
having the time to sit and paint
them. Margaret's garden had a
most inviting enclosed corner
with table and chairs, and
plants growing up the walls
around them.
Gay's garden and house on
a hillside in Dunedin has
several magical layers of garden.
On one level open to the sky the
next level features an enclosed
garden built around a tiled
courtyard, with small brick walls
to hold the plants in place.

One of Gay's Gardens

Walled Garden at Gay's

Details of Bags

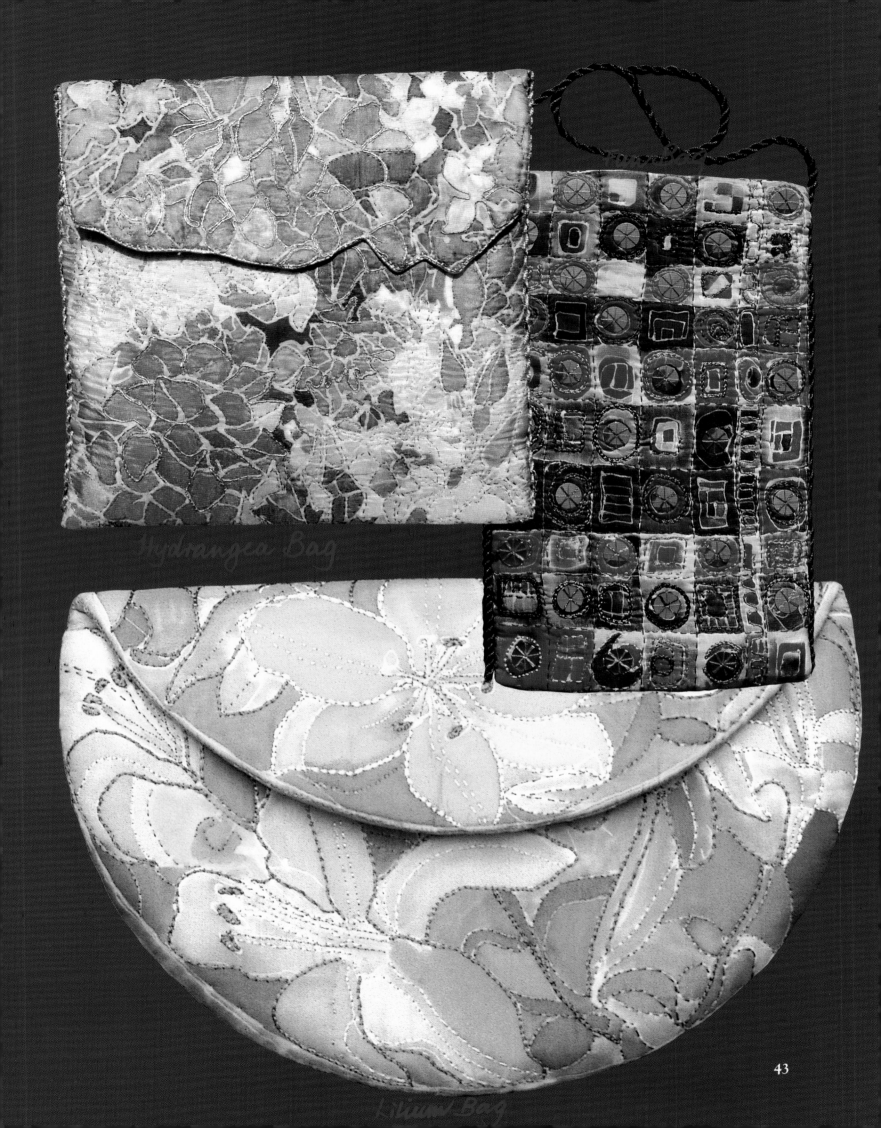

Hydrangea Bag

Lilium Bag

Harbours
Different techniques once more as
a new collection of drawings set new
directions. On a trip to the U.K. in the
sheltering harbours where the boats made such
strong patterns I had to sketch them. Staithes has
a very closed inner harbour where the boats are
carefully tied together so that they stay upright
as the tide goes out. This leads to the formation of
a tight network of shapes.

Polperro's inner harbour is seen through a side lane. In this collection of work I frequently found myself using the circle as the format. I also found I had to make a detailed design plan before I began the embroidery.

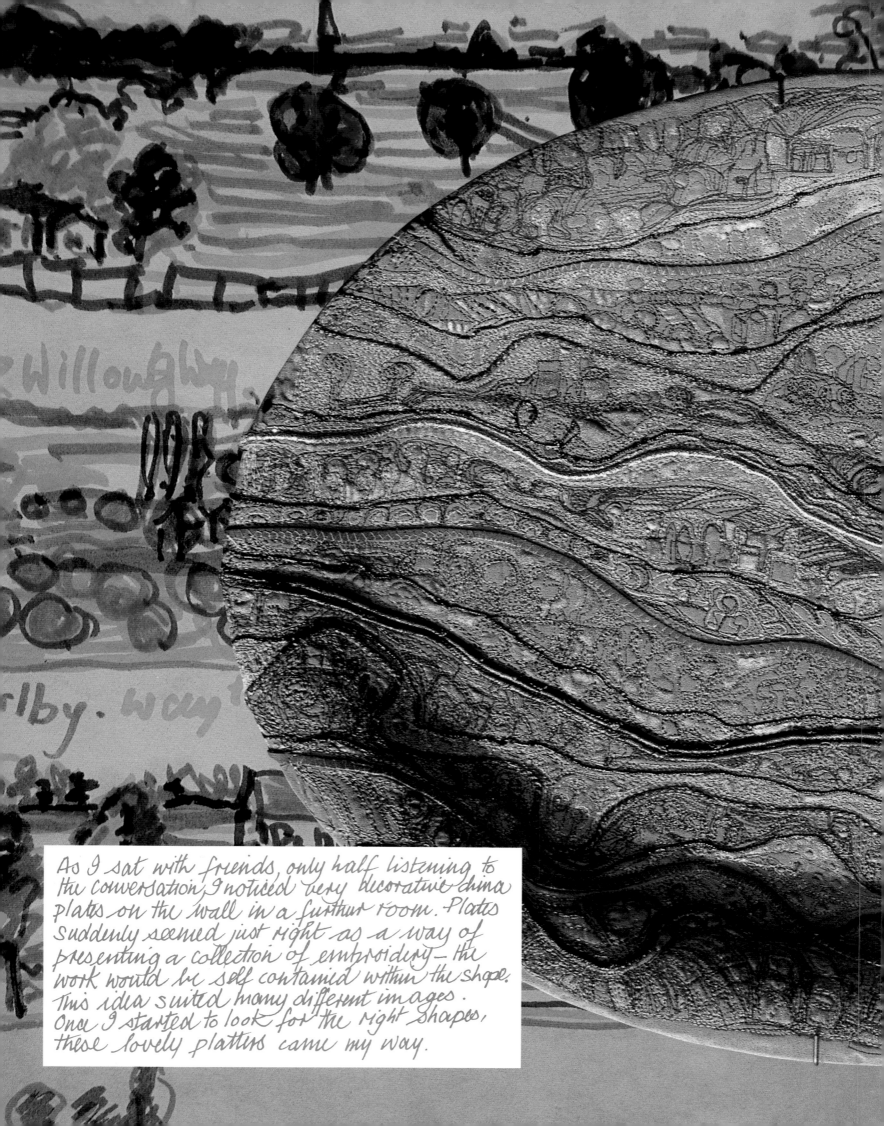

As I sat with friends, only half listening to the conversation, I noticed very decorative china plates on the wall in a further room. Plates suddenly seemed just right as a way of presenting a collection of embroidery — the work would be self contained within the shape. This idea suited many different images. Once I started to look for the right shapes, these lovely platters came my way.

Returning from York to Ely
This piece shows the many types of countryside,
the patterns of crops and trees, the endlessly
changing contours. In some places rolls of hay just
lying in the field made their own patterns.

The enclosed shapes of the platters were very suitable for such subjects as the theatre. 'The Jovial Crew' based on a mid-17th Century play by Richard Brome, was performed in the Swan Theatre at Stratford. Sitting close to the actors the Swan theatre-in-the-round meant my drawings took on an intimate quality. This in turn suited the restricted shape of the platter. The pattern of heads around the outside panel of the platter completes the design.

The Jovial Crew

Hay Fever

Hay Fever
This work I based
on a performance of
'Hay Fever' by Noel Coward
in the Lyric theatre in
Edinburgh where I
was very conscious of
the pillars, of their decorated
capitals. This time the
style of decoration with-
in the building became
a very important part
of the design.

The Rose Wall
It seemed to me that the rose was the dominant
flower throughout England. Roses climbed over
fences and arbours, there were separate rose
gardens everywhere. This rose was spectacular
as it climbed the side wall of a house, almost
reaching the roof.

Colosseum
This piece is
based on
drawings made
at the London
Colosseum just
before the curtain
went up on a
performance of
'The Magic Flute'.
The embroidery
was planned in
some detail in
my design book
before I
translated it
into its final
form.

Atmosphere at Sunset

Layers of Sunset

Composite Panels
This is a series
of fun works that
evolved from the
materials - sometimes
it is a good idea
to just enjoy your
materials and see
where they lead you.

Top Hill at Kingsand

A nostalgic trip back to childhood holidays. This spot in Cornwall has hardly changed: the same decorated houses, full of colour and pattern. The age of the houses, the variety of shape, the layers of paint that seem to wrap each house have a comfortable timeless quality.

54

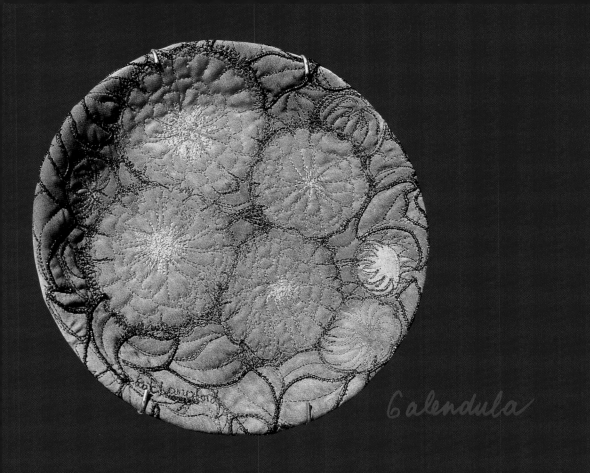

Calendula

Calendula and
Pale Poppies.

Whenever anyone
gives me flowers I
just have to sit
down and draw
them.
    There is always
such a freshness
of colour and shape
about the calendula
and as for poppies
who could imagine
such refinement
and delicacy of
colour.

Pale Poppies

Roses for her seventy-fifth
When visiting a friend in Perth
I was surprised to find it was
her birthday. Her house was full of roses.
Flowers en masse develope an amazing
richness which dominates ones visual field.
To capture the depth of colour I used crayon dyes
on linen, building up the colour until it filled the hollows in the fabric.

Richard Grows Dahlias

Such a glow of colour. My Cousin Richard has a passion for dahlias so the back garden is full of different varieties: from the largest blooms to the smallest pom-poms. There seemed to be new colours everytime I looked at the garden. (His wife Val doesn't like dahlias so he grows chrysanthemums for her.)

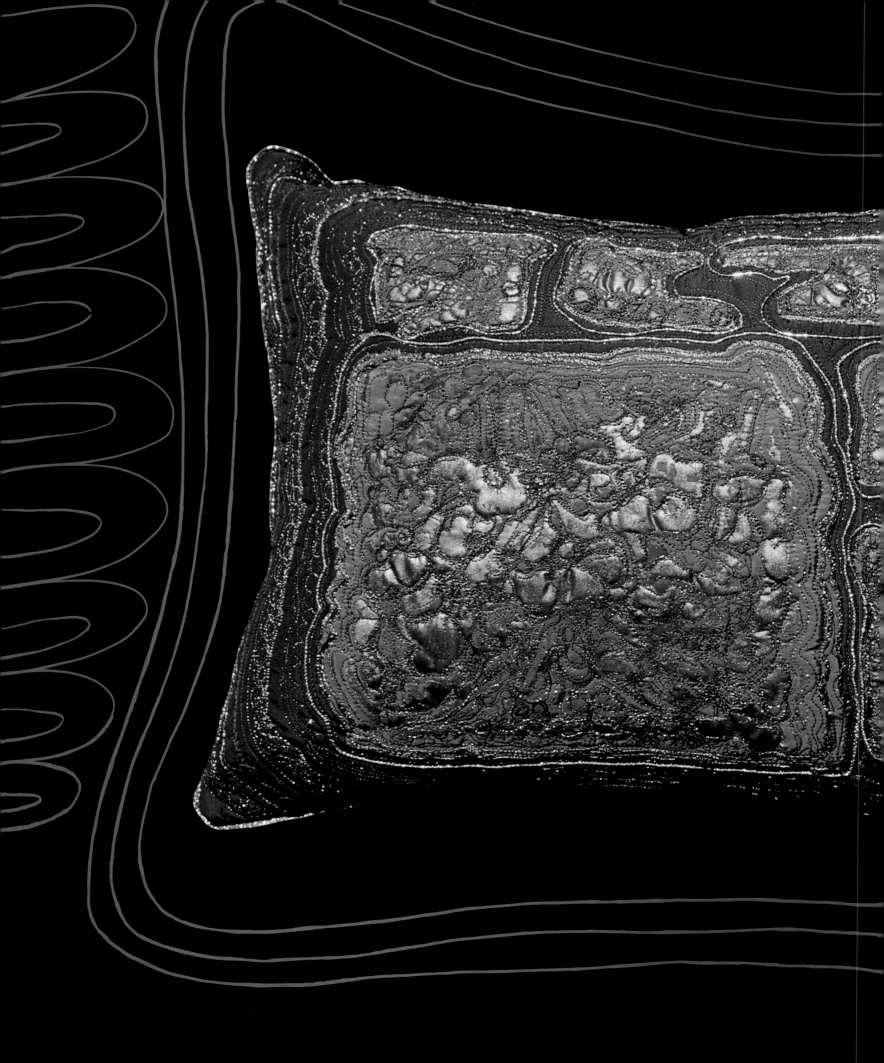

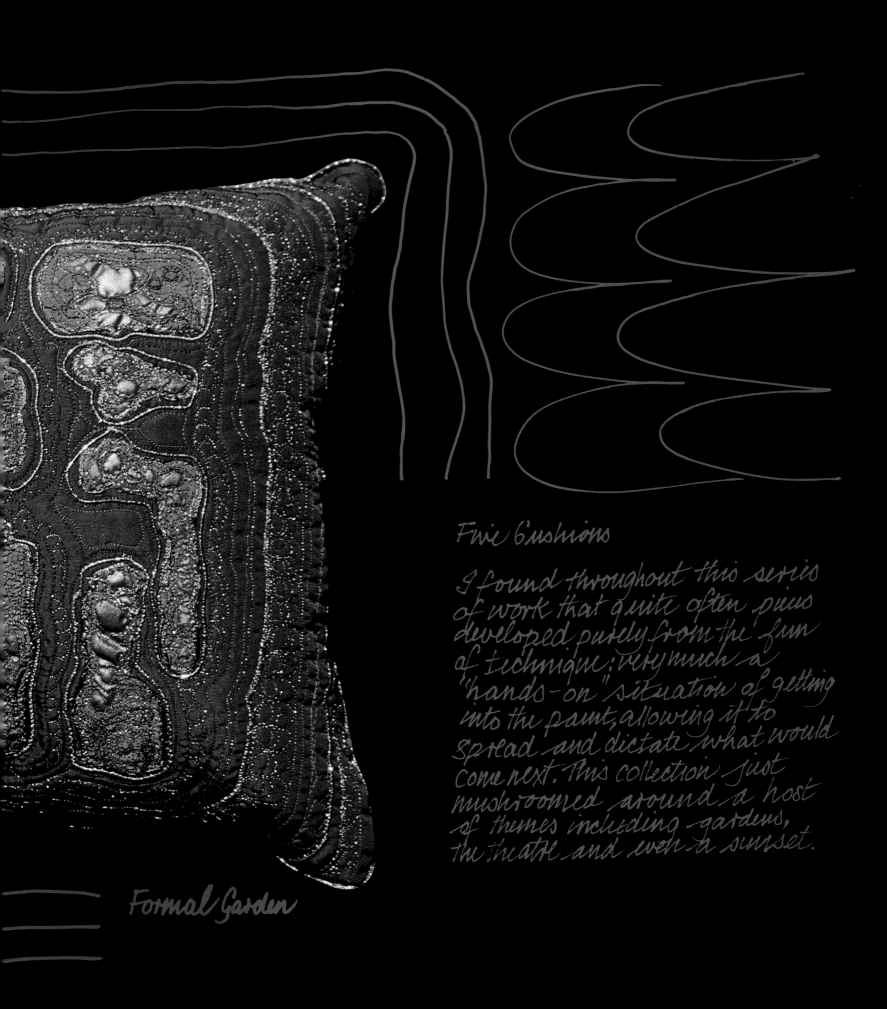

Formal Garden

Five Cushions

I found throughout this series
of work that quite often pieces
developed purely from the fun
of technique; very much a
"hands-on" situation of getting
into the paint, allowing it to
spread and dictate what would
come next. This collection just
mushroomed around a host
of themes including gardens,
the theatre and even a sunset.

Theatre Cushion

White Rose
detail

Runaway Garden cushion

Checkerboard twist cushion

Through the Window at Whitby

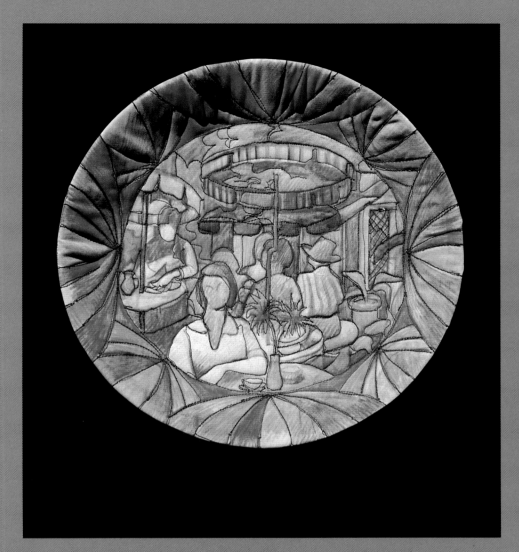

Fremantle Arts Centre
A drawing from the Fremantle Arts Centre where they painted each umbrella with individual decorations. A very lively effect with an enormous sense of vitality. Because it was a small courtyard, the figures fitted neatly into the centre of the plate and I was able to use the decorative umbrella shapes around the edge.

Franz Joseph

The work on these pages has mostly evolved from
the particular techniques used, and from the nature
of the fabrics. Both of them began as Monoprints with
gold paint, with sometimes an image in mind to
start with. But on other occasions I let the paint
do its own thing as it spread. Thus the final results
are dominated by the paint. 'Franz Joseph' was
developed from photographs and drawings of the
glacier. 'Broken Branches' just let the paint spread
and the design built around the fine shapes.

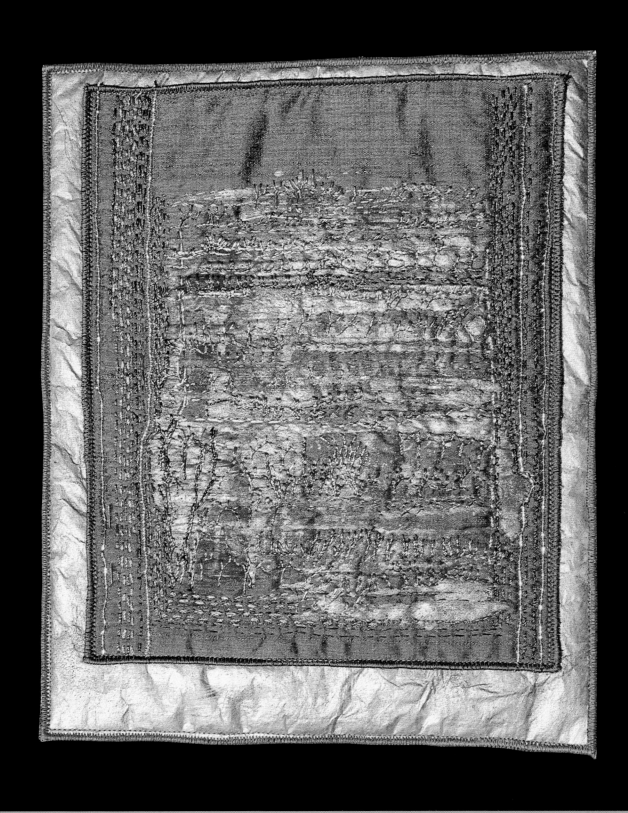

Broken Branches

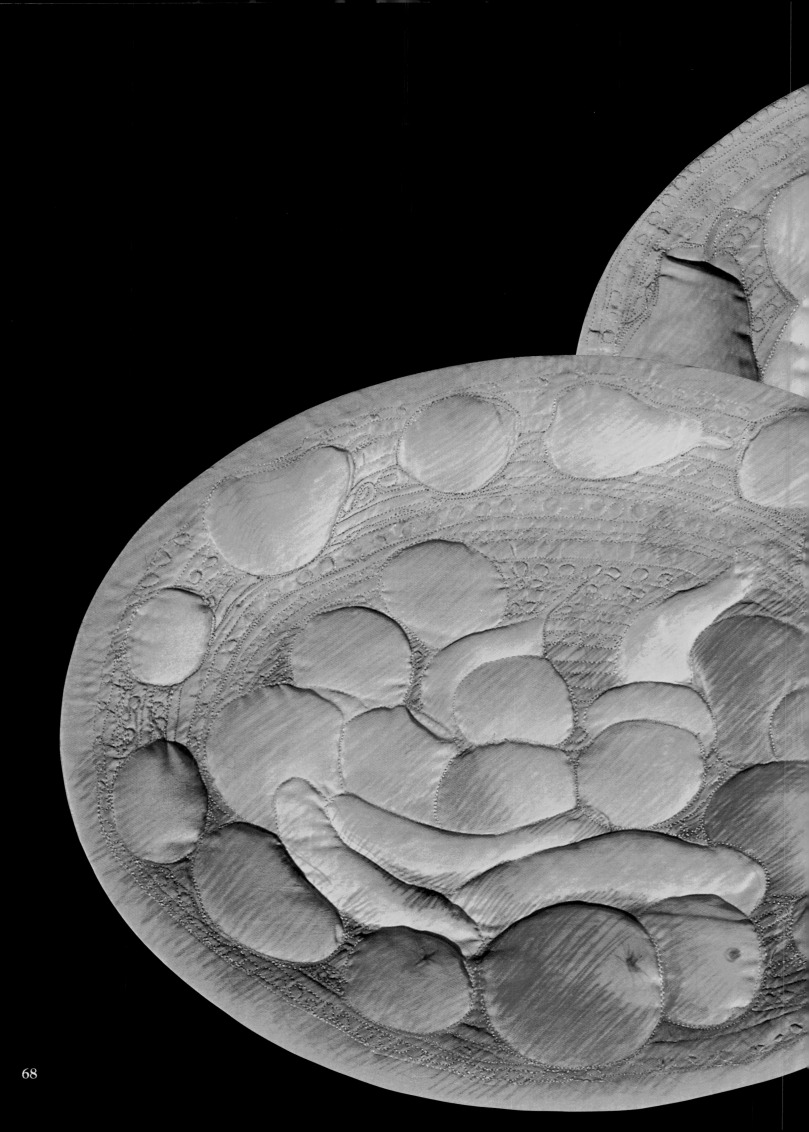

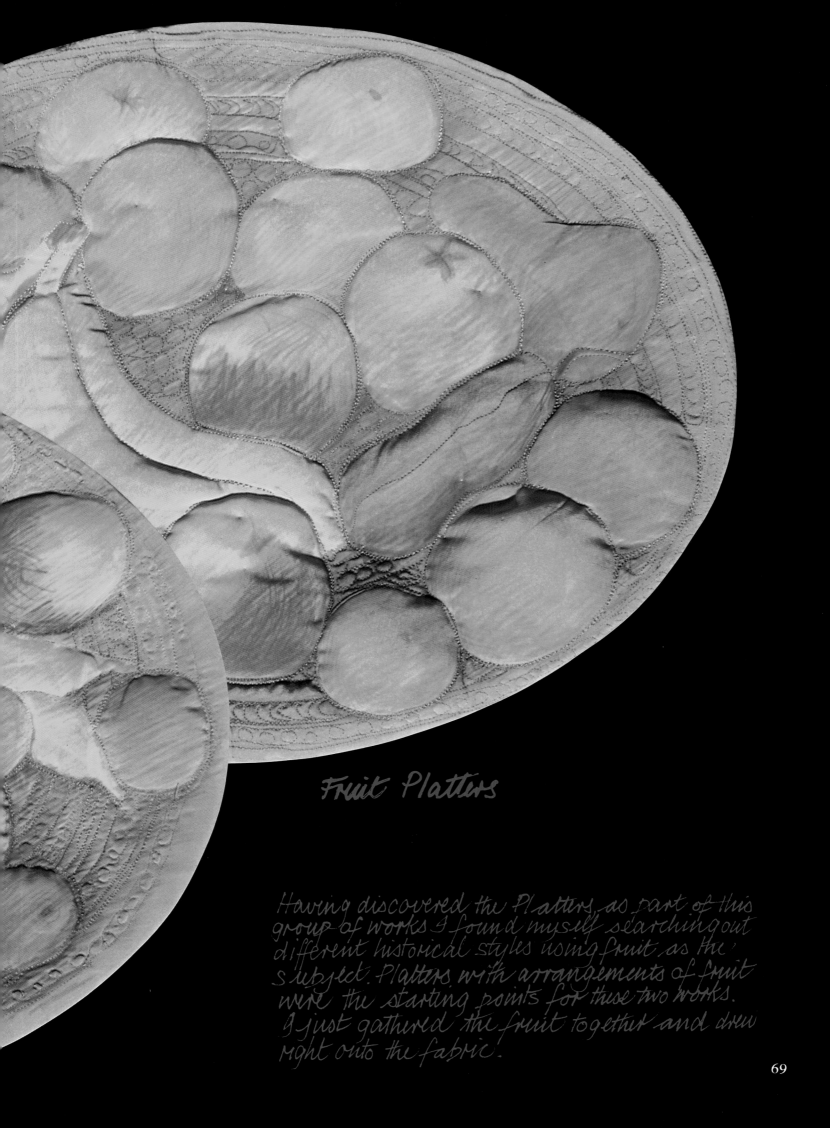

Fruit Platters

Having discovered the Platters, as part of this
group of works I found myself searching out
different historical styles using fruit as the
subject. Platters with arrangements of fruit
were the starting points for these two works.
I just gathered the fruit together and drew
right onto the fabric.

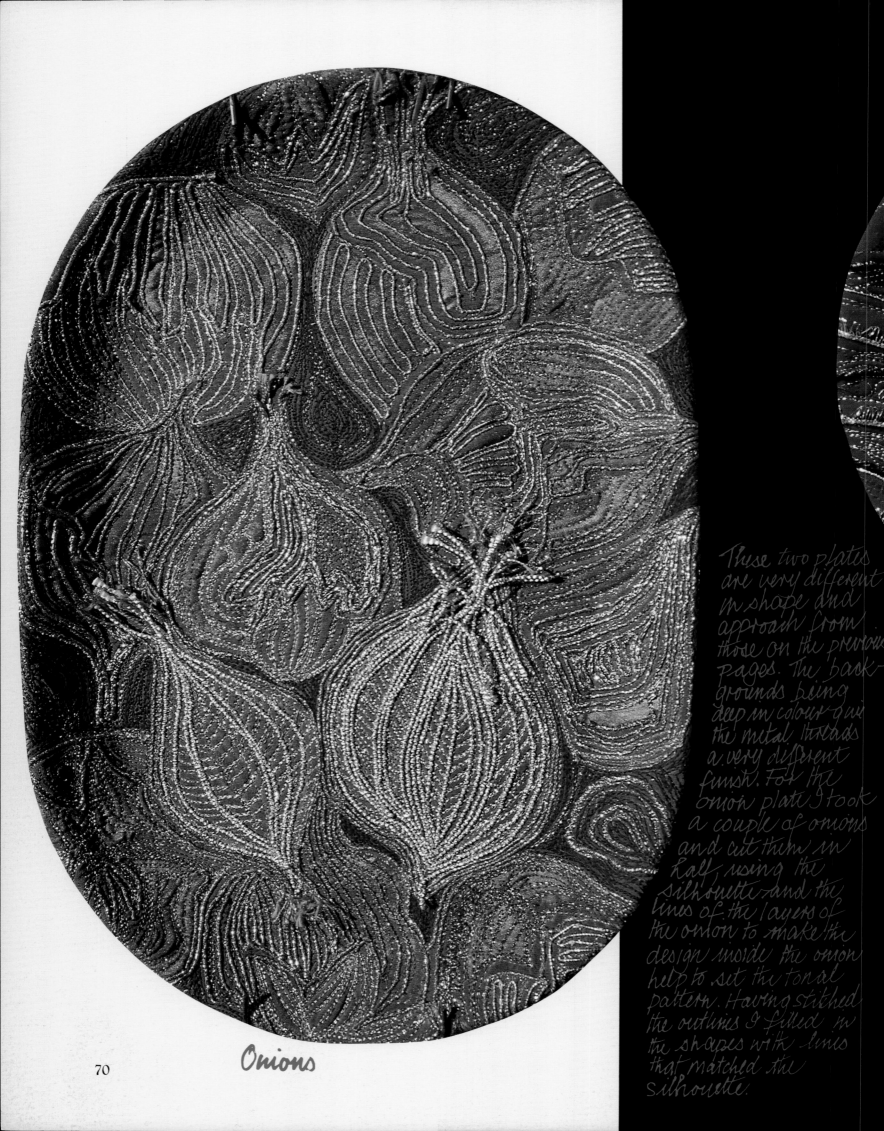

Onions

These two plates are very different in shape and approach from those on the previous pages. The back grounds being deep in colour give the metal threads a very different finish. For the onion plate I took a couple of onions and cut them in half, using the silhouette and the lines of the layers of the onion to make the design inside the onion help to set the tonal pattern. Having stitched the outlines I filled in the shapes with lines that matched the silhouette.

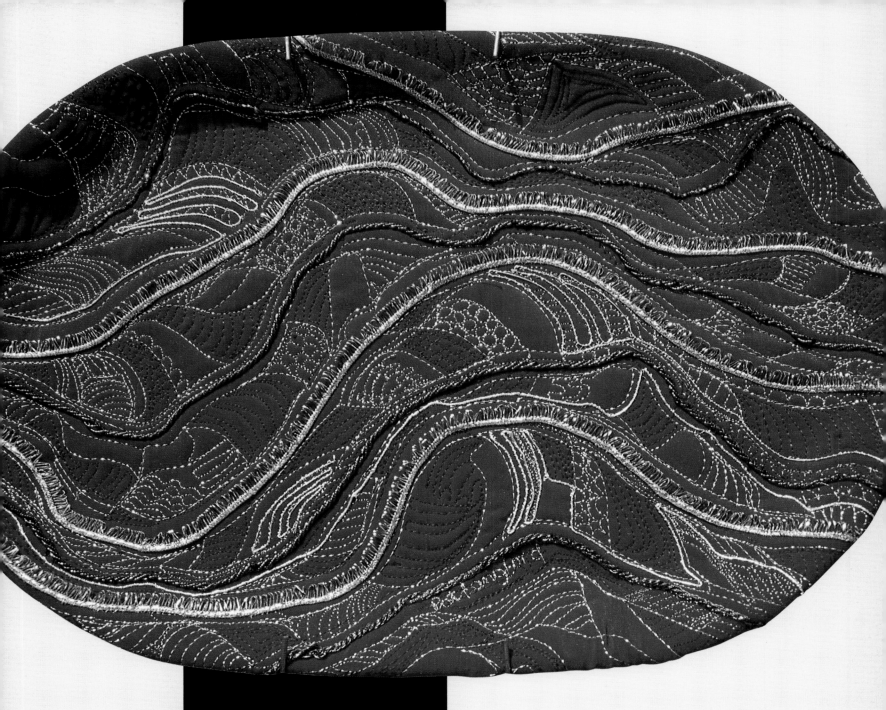

Torquay

Again the depth of
colour was just
right for the red soil
of Devon. Rhythmic
lines of silver cord
suggested the
rolling hills covered
in endless patterns
of the fields.

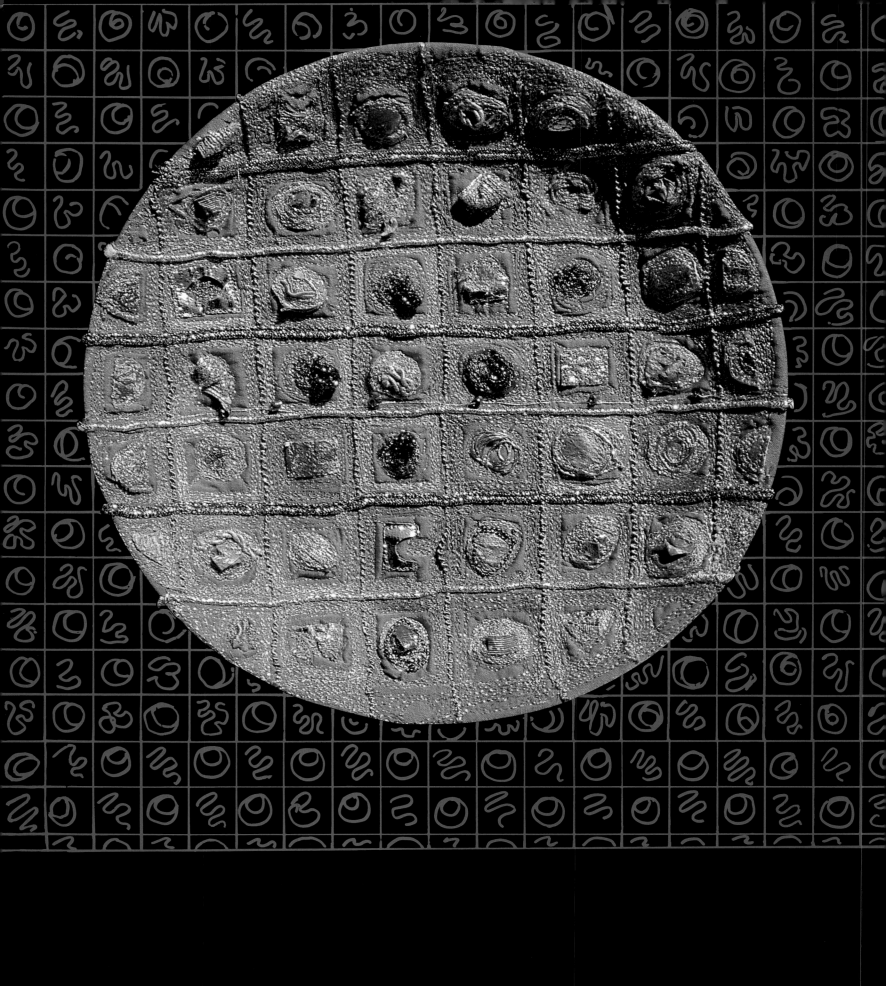

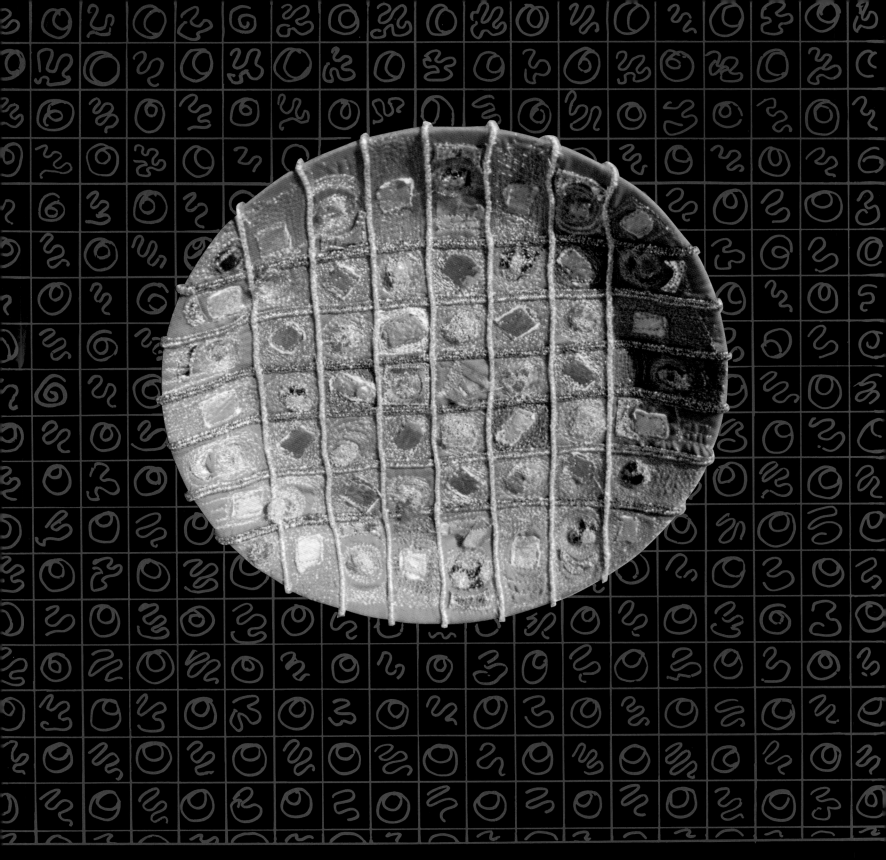

Golden Images

The joy of texture and touch is realised in
these works. An unexpected treasure-trove of
metallic cords in a fabric-cum-haberdashery
shop in Mullumbimby just had to be used.
The myriad different cords only needed these
geometric shapes to show them at their best
with many small textured centres.

Eastbourne
Amongst the many different
places I visited in the U.K.
I was fascinated by the Victorian
piers still surviving, all well
maintained, with restored areas
of decoration, lampposts and
much wrought iron in evidence,
little shelters and deck chairs
in corners. Looking through my
sketchbooks I became intrigued
by the idea of making a
set of plates on the subject.

Gooindi
What a wonderful spot to come back to at the end of a hot day in Kakadu. Returning from Yellow Waters to the covered coolness of the pub to sit under the cool slatted roof and discuss the day's activities. The enclosed area with filtered light seemed to ask for a fine stitch to interpret the mood.

Exmoor

Heather on Exmoor, such subtle colours as it blankets the hillsides. A very different range of colour asking for special treatment, constantly changing as I travelled across the moors. Broken colour was essential to capture the changes.

79

Techniques

Magic Tree, p. 8, 70 cm x 56 cm (27½" x 22")

At the time of preparing the work for this exhibition I was very involved in silk painting. Of the many silk painting dyes on the market I find Le Prince to be particularly good colours and easy to use. I worked with Habutat silk which was stretched tightly on a frame, using masking tape to keep the silk in place. It is important to stretch the fabric on the grain, making sure it lines up parallel to the edge of the frame. The outlines were drawn with gutta to separate the colours. After finishing the painting the silk was taken off the frame and the colours fixed with a hot iron.

To prepare the work for stitching, the silk was backed with a layer of thin wadding and calico ready for quilting. Some works were quilted by hand, others on the machine.

Valleys Beyond, p. 9, 58 cm x 40 cm (23" x 16")

Metal threads were used to enrich the small centre piece: these were sometimes couched by hand. The quilting was then machined onto the canvas background. The drawings were done with Polychromos, adding rich colour to the background. The drawing helps to suggest the endless space around the smaller details.

Hills that Run Forever, p. 10, 68 cm x 56 cm (27" x 22")

The three panels in this work were drawn onto one piece of silk which was first stretched on an embroidery frame. The pieces were quilted with lines of machine stitching following the lines of the drawing.

After adding rows of straight stitching, then satin stitch, around the edges of each rectangle, the pieces were cut into strips and attached to the canvas. The direction of the machine lines across the sky help to further the sense of distance and add to the continuity of hill and sky.

How Can I Take In So Much? detail, p. 12, 300 cm x 96 cm (118" x 37¾")

This work brings together all the techniques used in this series. I used small quilted pieces, coloured papers, specially dyed silk and other coloured fabrics. I drew the river and its banks onto the background with the coloured pencils and painted many small pieces of silk. Some were bonded right onto the background, others were quilted and machined, with some hand stitching. These were then machined onto the background in prominent places.

Timber Creek, p. 20, 66 cm x 60 cm (26" x 24")
For this piece I have used reverse applique, a building technique, with four layers of fabric which were machined onto the background fabric. Dark green comes first, then blue, red and fawn. I used my original colour sketch as a starting point as it was important to have the tonal arrangement worked out first. The technique dictates the style of the work. I found myself constantly cutting a bit more fabric away. The colour of the satin stitch covering the edges is important to give clarity to the design shapes.

The Devil's Marbles

Three Drawings, p. 22, 28 cm x 38 cm (11" x 15")
These three works are taken from drawings made from the bus as we travelled through Kakadu. This time I worked straight from the sketchbook. I made clear tracings and transferred them to a soft woollen fabric by pinning the tracing to the fabric, tacking the drawing through the tracing, then tearing the paper away.

I framed each piece in a cardboard frame, which is light to carry. Each piece is backed with a layer of fine wadding, then calico. These works were all stitched by hand, using mostly shiny threads and perle threads in a variety of stitches.

Golden Grass

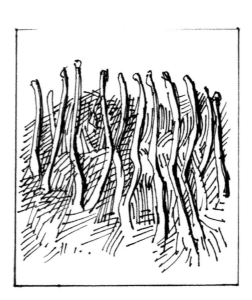

Waving Grass at Jabiru

The Suggestion of Light, p. 14, 44 cm x 46 cm (17½" x 18")

In this group I used paper as my background. Watercolour paper, hand made paper, etching paper seemed to be important as a medium to capture the wonderful morning light of the Flinders. Pieces of coloured and dyed fabric were stitched onto the paper. Torn and rolled papers were also machined on.

Wonderful edges and layering effects are created by tearing thick hand made papers. Something you have to watch while tearing this sort of paper is just how interesting you make the edge. The direction in which you tear often dictates the kind of edge you get.

The black line drawings made on the top of all the materials, both papers and cloth, tie all the parts together.

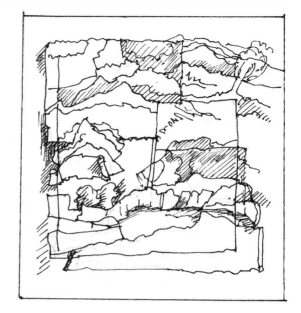

Rich Red of the Olgas, p. 16, 54 cm x 47 cm (21¼" x 18½")

The same fabrics were used for many of the works in this series about the Olgas. The quiet green background is a polyester cotton supported by calico. This time I had the drawing beside me as I cut the layers of pink, orange and red, pinned them down and machined from the centre out. Dark reds were then attached and a lot of machine stitching was used to pattern the shapes. Small pieces of bright red fabric were cut up and added, along with short lengths of thread and wools. This piece grew and developed as the work went along. Watching the tonal pattern, I added small dark areas here and there to emphasise the contours. Hand stitching was added at the end to enrich the surface.

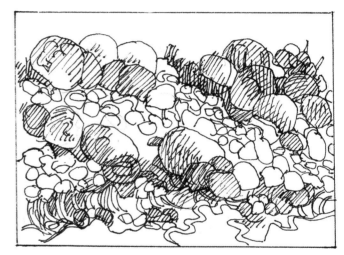

Pink Light at Waterfall, p. 24, 70 cm x 56 cm (27½" x 22")

The same green fabric was used as background for this work but this time strips of many different colours were pinned across the green and machined. The basic shapes of the trees were added next. Then endless circles of machine stitching were layered on top of each other, building a surface of broken colour. I kept adding more stitching until I had arrived at the colours which suggested the broken light on the landscape.

Home of the Spinifex Mouse, p. 26, 46 cm x 41 cm (18" x 16")
I used dark colours for the inside of the circle and gradually worked in the lighter top colours. Couching the lighter threads to the work to stand up in front of the background, I sometimes added two or even three threads to increase the relief.

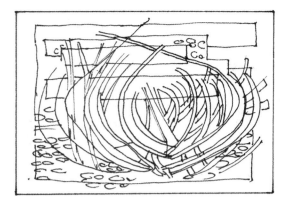

Spinifex Circle, p. 27, 46 cm x 41 cm (18" x 16")
Because the ground was very hard around the spinifex grass, I didn't use any padding here, just a piece of calico to support the fabric. Small pieces of organza were stitched down first. I then searched for different kinds of threads to cut up in short lengths which I attached in bundles to suggest the grass, plus many other small pieces of materials.

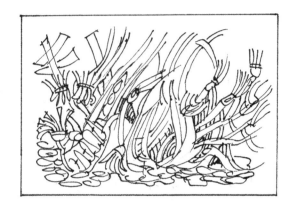

YOLANDE'S WINDOWS: Series, pp. 28–34
To me the most exciting aspect of this group of works is the constant changes of materials and techniques. I gathered all the gold kid and related coloured papers, all within the gold and blue colour scheme, that I could lay my hands on and then had fun interpreting this small drawing in many different arrangements to suggest different moods.

Kitchen Window, p. 29, 32 cm x 38 cm (12½" x 15")
Gold kid, one of the richest materials possible, was used as a background. It helps to reveal the quality of light in this corner. The window was cut into the kid and the blue papers were laid behind. After a lot of machining copper gold leaf was added for the highlights.

Clutter in the Window, p. 29, 32 cm x 38 cm (12½" x 15")
Also uses gold kid. This time smaller windows were cut and an etching laid behind. Just a suggestion of quilting is used for the window recess.

After the Party, p. 30, 32 cm x 38 cm (12½" x 15")
Uses layers of different coloured blue paper with bands of gold, all machined together.
Metal threads and gold leaf were added as final touches.

Through the Hatch, p. 34, 33 cm x 43 cm (13" x 17")
One more drawing from Yolande's house, *Through the Hatch* uses a very different technique. Soft baby blanketing was a strange purchase as I had no idea when I bought it how I was going to use it. Suddenly one day puff paint and blanket came together and I found myself drawing my design straight on to the blanket with the puff paint. Because of the depth through the hatch into the room next door, I used three layers, cutting through each one and finally right through in the centre. The pink organza was then pinned over the work and all the lines of the design were machined. I then cut the organza away to reveal the white blanket. I then laid the blue organza down and machined around all the lines again, cutting back the blue where necessary to allow the pink to show through.

Deep Window Space, p. 33, 32 cm x 38 cm (12½" x 15")
Again uses a non-reflective surface with different papers machined down and gold paint with gold leaf applied before cutting an irregular edge.

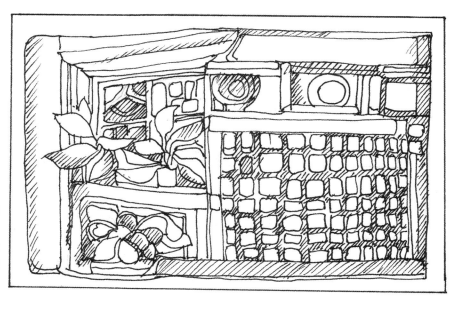

The Corner of the Lounge Room, p. 35, 50 cm x 40 cm (20" x 16")
Uses the same colours but in reverse, showing pink organza on the top, the final result being quite a different colour arrangement.

Double Image, p. 32, 64 cm x 38 cm (20" x 16")
The two parts of *Double Image* are on different backgrounds. The left-hand one uses paper. This time the windows were just outlined by machine with the highlight of the glass in painted gold paper. The right-hand side is worked on a non-reflective surface. This time the glass of the windows is suggested by gold kid and gold paper.

NEW ZEALAND GARDENS: Series, pp. 36–38
61 cm x 46 cm (24" x 18")

This series of garden works really exploited the technique of layering and the texture of blanket. In *Margaret's Garden* I found myself cutting back through many layers and adding small pieces of red silk or yellow, machining and cutting again. The table-top had far too much paint and I shaved off some of the surface to give an interesting texture.

In *Gay's Garden* I found I had to lay another piece of blue organza over the sky to give it distance and density, and add much more paint to the blanketing to give a crunchy surface.

Decorative Bags, p. 40

These bags are all examples of silk painting. Each bag has a very different design: some come from flower drawings in my sketchbook while others are drawn right onto the silk from the bowl of flowers sitting on the table. All of them have been drawn with gutta first, then the spaces filled in.

The hydrangea bag is made from one piece of fabric stretched tightly on a picture frame. I placed a bowl of hydrangeas and fuchsias on the table in front of me. Starting at one end I carefully drew the flowers with gutta, filling all the area of the bag as I moved across the fabric.I then filled in the colour just as you would a watercolour After heat-fixing I tacked on a fine layer of wadding and calico. These bags are all hand quilted.

To keep the hydrangea bag and the fun bag smooth I rolled them around a cardboard lunch-wrap tube when not working on them. When the quilting was completed I added the silver thread to give the work an extra finish. I cut an irregular edge across the front of the hydrangea bag.

I dyed the linings to match each bag, adding cords made in the colours of the bags to complete the work. The small fun bag divided into squares with designs in each space has sequins and beads as a finish.

The lilium bag, which was worked in a frame, followed the same procedure as the previous bags. This time I used backstitch to outline some of the flowers with couching, plus bullion knots for the stamens. I dyed the lining of this bag to match, then quilted the same design over the lining in a self colour.

Hydrangea Bag

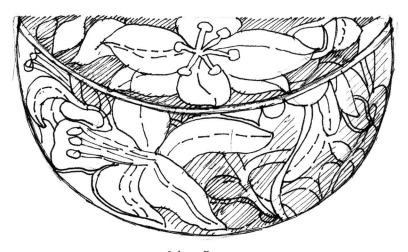

Lilium Bag

Fun Bag

HARBOURS, p. 44

With works like *Staithes* I had to plan the design in considerable detail before I started. At the time I happened to have a pile of Irish linens in the cupboard just waiting to be used—four colours, pale blue, yellow, green and pink—in a very fine weave. I stretched the fabric in a frame and drew the design on with Pentel fabric crayons, which must be ironed to fix the dyes. The crayons must be used quite heavily to get good strong colour. The linen did not need wadding to support it, just calico to add strength while machining.

Staithes

Polperro

Returning from York to Ely, p. 46, 50 cm x 35 cm (20" x 13¾")

This piece was worked on microfibre, a relatively new fabric which comes in a wide variety of colours, from soft and quiet to rich and deep. The fabric was backed with a fine wadding and calico, all three fabrics being pinned from the centre out.

The gold cords were machined on first, each line couched down with a zig-zag stitch. Once these lines were established I worked the landscapes with free machining, alternating one colour against the next, keeping a strong emphasis on one colour in each space and using many different drawings from the sketchbook.

'*The Jovial Crew*' and '*Hay Fever*', p. 48,
50 cm x 35 cm (20" x 13¾")
Both these pieces are worked on
microfibre, each having a richly coloured background. The fabric was
stretched on a piece of board before
starting. The drawings were done with
Polychromos coloured pencils, which
come in a very good colour range. After fixing the colour, I machined the
fabrics, working from the centre out.
This technique is important because it
stops the fabric from puckering.

In '*The Jovial Crew*' I used just navy
blue and purple for the machine
stitching; '*Hay Fever*' uses mostly warm
matching colours.

The Rose Wall (detail), p. 50, 84 cm x 54 cm (33" x 21¼")
Having chosen the fabric and colours for the flower heads, I transferred the
gold paint onto the background fabric by doing a monoprint. Using a thicker
wadding I then quilted this part to give the suggestion of a brick or stone wall.

The flowers were worked on water-soluble fabric, two layers stretched in
an embroidery hoop to give extra strength while stitching.

I used gold and copper metallic thread and Isofel in a metafil needle with
the machine embroidery, using the same threads in the bobbin. The next step
was to dip the fabric into a bowl of water to dissolve, leaving the flowers as a
kind of embroidered applique to be machined onto the background.

Coloseum, p. 52, 55 cm x 54 cm (21½" x 21")
This piece kept closely to my original sketchbook design. Again I
have used linen, stitched and crayoned with just two colours this
time, gold and blue, as background to the gold threads. Marlitt, a
shiny thread, gives a rich quality to the stitching. The work is mostly
done in running stitch, taken across the work diagonally to suggest
the movement of light in the theatre. The outlines around the col-
umns, and other lines, were couched down.

Composite Panels, p. 53, 62 cm 52 cm (24½" x 20½")
These works on small pieces of canvas were started when I felt the
need for some hand stitching to work on while travelling! I painted
a number of squares with gold paint, added strips of canvas and small
pieces of organza. I then added small areas of stitches.

   The background was textured and coloured with copper and gold
paint as a monoprint onto organza, which gave a misty effect when
laid on the background.

Top Hill at Kingsand, p. 54, 26 cm (10¼") diameter
Calendula and *Pale Poppies*, p. 55, 26 cm (10¼") diameter
Each of these three works uses the same technique—transfer dying
onto microfibre with Crayola fabric crayons. These crayons are very
easy to use. The design shapes are drawn onto paper which is laid
face-down onto the fabric and ironed. You need to experiment with
these crayons and become familiar with them before using them on
a final piece as the colour on the paper does not give a true indica-
tion of the density of colour that appears on the fabric. Light wadding and calico were used to support the fabric. Each piece was machined with silky threads.

   In *Calendula* I used antique metallic thread as a final touch.

Top Hill at Kingsand

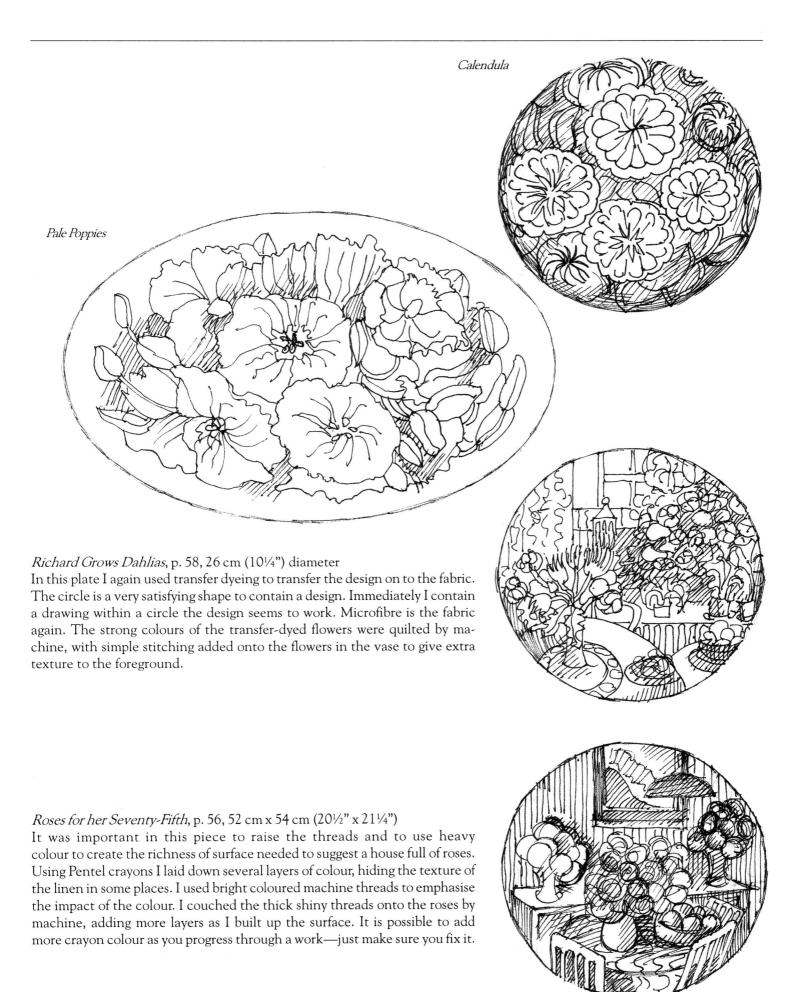

Calendula

Pale Poppies

Richard Grows Dahlias, p. 58, 26 cm (10¼") diameter
In this plate I again used transfer dyeing to transfer the design on to the fabric. The circle is a very satisfying shape to contain a design. Immediately I contain a drawing within a circle the design seems to work. Microfibre is the fabric again. The strong colours of the transfer-dyed flowers were quilted by machine, with simple stitching added onto the flowers in the vase to give extra texture to the foreground.

Roses for her Seventy-Fifth, p. 56, 52 cm x 54 cm (20½" x 21¼")
It was important in this piece to raise the threads and to use heavy colour to create the richness of surface needed to suggest a house full of roses. Using Pentel crayons I laid down several layers of colour, hiding the texture of the linen in some places. I used bright coloured machine threads to emphasise the impact of the colour. I couched the thick shiny threads onto the roses by machine, adding more layers as I built up the surface. It is possible to add more crayon colour as you progress through a work—just make sure you fix it.

FIVE CUSHIONS: Series, pp. 60–62

Four of these cushions started out as simple monoprints using mostly Jo Sonja's acrylic paints. I use a piece of glass as my printing surface, but a piece of formica or any smooth surface which is easy to clean will do. Although acrylic paints are water-soluble it is always easier to clean it off the work surface before it dries.

Squeeze the paint onto the glass and spread it with a palette knife or spatula or even a piece of thick card. Draw a design into the paint or texture it with a comb or the end of a brush. Lay the fabric down onto the paint and smooth it out gently from the centre so it picks up the paint. Peel it off carefully, lay flat and let the paint dry. Support the fabric with fine wadding and calico ready for stitching.

Formal Garden Cushion, 50 cm x 38 cm (20" x 15")

The monoprint on pale blue fabric was quite heavily patterned with machine stitching and then cut into small irregular shapes that were re-assembled. More machining was added, particularly around the edges, and lines repeating the outlines of the shapes were taken out to the edge of the cushion.

When attaching one piece of fabric to another, particularly a large area like the pale blue onto the darker blue, it is a good idea to machine from the centre out. I machined in the same places I had stitched previously to avoid adding confusing lines.

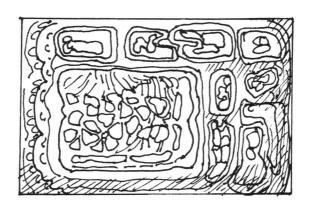

Theatre Cushion, 46 cm x 38 cm (18" x 15")

Decorations from the theatre were the inspiration for this cushion. Beginning from the centre and working outwards I have machined different coloured Russian braids on their edges, making them stand up. I carried the shapes out to the edge of the piece of brown fabric, which was then stitched to the blue background, with the couching and stitching extended right out to the edge of the cushion.

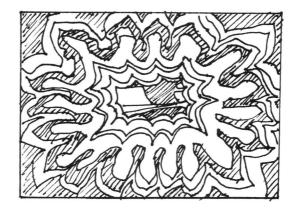

White Rose Cushion, 48 cm x 38 cm (18" x 15")

The shapes produced by the monoprint suggested the large and small areas of a bunch of roses. By machining around the shapes I gradually built them up into a group of flower heads. Adding machine couching around the shapes was the next step. I then machined the background into small patterns to flatten those areas against the roses. Gold threads were couched around the rectangle, more paint was added and further lines of couching were laid. Parallel lines of quilting in self colour were stitched to the edge of the cushion. A fine machine made cord was hand stitched around the edge.

Runaway Garden Cushion, 48 cm x 38 cm (19" x 15")
This cushion began with two monoprints which were cut into new shapes and stitched to the dull green background fabric. The Russian braid and other threads were stitched on by hand, and machine running stitch and some lacing was added. The orange colours were important as points of emphasis in the overall colour scheme. The green fabric was machined onto the blue fabric with a couched line covering the join.

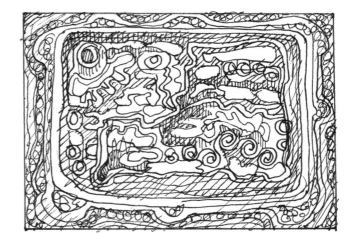

Checkerboard Sunset Cushion, 48 cm x 40 cm (19" x 15")
This cushion combined many different techniques, starting with the small canvaswork piece in the centre. I then set up two pieces of water-soluble fabric in a frame with the canvaswork as the starting point and machined heavy lines from the edge of the canvas outwards. Hand made paper which was already painted gold was attached to this grid. I just continued to work out to the next square, adding Greek metallic braid and more paper.

Because I had used paper I just dampened the work to remove the water-soluble fabric and laid it on a towel to dry. I then machined the work on to a piece of organza laid on top of deep blue fabric. This cushion is finished with a piping cord.

RIGHT:
Through the Window at Whitby, p. 65, 28 cm x 33 cm (11" x 13")
This plate illustrates Polychromos at their best, allowing the fine drawing to convey the detail of this fascinating window from inside the coffee shop.

Lunch at Fremantle Arts Centre, p. 65, 26 cm (10¼") diameter
The shape of the plate suggested a decorative edge as a surround to the design. The decorative umbrellas, their undersides painted with large reclining figures, seemed to become the dominant element of the design.

Franz Joseph, p. 66, 38 cm x 28 cm (15" x 11")
Broken Branches, p. 67, 32 cm 42 cm (12½" x 16½")

These works developed from the suggestions made by the accidental shapes in the monoprints. *Broken Branches* was hand stitched using mostly fly stitch, buttonhole stitch and running stitch. *Franz Joseph* was machine quilted, taking the lines around the mountain shapes. Both of these works were then machined onto fine hand painted paper before the final borders were added.

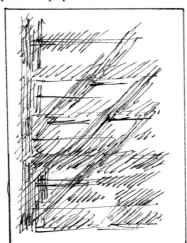

Fruit Platters, p. 68, 50 cm x 35 cm (20" x 13¼")

These two pieces of embroidery both use microfibre with Polychromos to build the drawing. The character of the fabric behind the coloured pencils gives a velvet quality to the work. When I organised the padding I cut extra pieces of wadding to raise the fruit from the plate, placing them between the top and the calico. After I finished the machining I added further pieces of wadding behind the work to increase the relief before attaching it to the plate.

Onions, p. 70, 22 cm x 32 cm (8½" x 12½")

Both this work and *Torquay* are dominated by the shape of the plates.

With the sliced onions beside me I painted some areas of colour on to the fabric. When it was dry I just enjoyed couching down many different threads around the shapes. I used knitting cottons, gold and copper twists, and other suitable threads. I then machined the negative spaces between the onions with dark red and copper metallic threads.

Torquay, p. 71, 32 cm x 22 cm (12½" x 8½")
The wonderful silver cord was the starting point, with the colour of the fabric being perfect for the red soil of Devon. The cord was stitched down first, fitting the shape of the plate. The metallic machine threads plus the Jap silver and twists enrich the surface of the fabric with the many patterns of small fields.

Golden Images 1 and 2, p. 72, 26 cm (10¼") diameter
The textured details of these two plates were first assembled on water-soluble fabric using many small pieces of cord, paper, gold kid, gold threads, ribbon. Again because of the paper I just dampened the piece carefully to dissolve the water-soluble fabric. The cords were laid across the fabric to set up the grid, then the textured pieces stitched into the spaces. More stitching was added to make the surface as rich as possible.

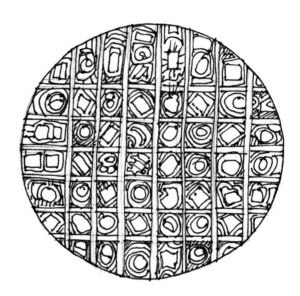

Eastbourne, p. 74, 22 cm (8¾") diameter
Because of the pictorial content of this set the works needed to be treated very simply. They were drawn with Polychromos pencils and then machine quilted.

Cooindi, p. 76, 40 cm x 30 cm (16" x 11¾")
These works are taken from tracings of my original sketches. The tracings were tacked to the linen and carefully stitched along each line so that I had accurate drawings to work with. I used just one thread in simple running stitch, laying different colours beside each other and keeping the direction of the stitches diagonal across the work to suggest the light.

Exmoor, p. 78, 56 cm x 38 cm (22" x 15")
These works also started with monoprints. As this is a textured fabric the paint spread in between the ridges of the material, creating a very different surface, with the different coloured areas suggesting the heather on the moor. I stitched around these shapes, taking most of the stitching in one direction, changing angles with the changes in the landscape. After the centre was finished I added rows of fine running stitch as an outside mount.

Sissinghurst, p. 80, 50 cm (20") diameter
After suggesting the design with crayon onto green linen, I cut many threads into short lengths and stitched them into place. Many flower heads were created by machining continuous threads on top of themselves into a circle, just turning the hoop as I zig-zagged.
The flower heads in the foreground are built up from many strands of threads held with machine stitching and some hand stitching. The circle of work was then stitched on to a green polyester taffeta which was textured with machine embroidery.

Index